Living with Discernment in the End Times

KAY ARTHUR
DAVID LAWSON
BOB VEREEN

HARVEST HOUSE™ PUBLISHERS

EUGENE, OREGON

Cover by Koechel Peterson & Associates, Inc., Minneapolis, Minnesota

The New Inductive Study Series
LIVING WITH DISCERNMENT IN THE END TIMES

Copyright © 2002 by Precept Ministries
Published by Harvest House Publishers
Eugene, Oregon 97402
www.harvesthousepublishers.com

Library of Congress Cataloging-in-Publication Data
Arthur, Kay, 1933–
 Living with discernment in the end times / Kay Arthur, David Lawson, Bob Vereen.
  p. cm. — (The new inductive study series)
 ISBN 978-0-7369-0446-9 (pbk.)
 ISBN 978-0-7369-3611-8 (eBook)
 1. Bible. N.T. Peter—Study and teaching. 2. Bible. N.T. Jude—Study and teaching.
 3. Christian life—Biblical teaching. I. Lawson, David. II. Vereen, Bob. III. Title.
BS2795.55 .A78 2002
227' .92'0071—dc21

               2002005631

Printed in the United States of America

13 14 15 16 / BP-VS / 15 14 13 12 11

CONTENTS

∾∾∾∾

How to Get Started...

FIRST

As you study the books of 1 and 2 Peter and Jude, you will need four things in addition to this book:

1. A Bible that you are willing to mark in. Marking is essential because it is an integral part of the learning process and will help you remember and retain what you learned. An ideal Bible for this purpose is *The New Inductive Study Bible (NISB)*. The *NISB*, available in the New American Standard Version, comes in a single-column text format with larger, easy-to-read type, and is ideal for marking. The page margins are wide and blank for note-taking.

The *NISB* is unique among all study Bibles in that it has instructions for studying each book of the Bible, but it does not contain any commentary on the text. The *NISB* isn't compiled from any particular theological stance because its purpose is to teach you how to discern truth for yourself through the inductive method of study. Inductive Bible study simply means that the Bible itself is the primary source for study. (The various charts and maps that you will find in this study guide are taken from the *NISB*.) Whatever Bible you use, just know you will need to mark in it, which brings us to the second item you will need.

2. A fine-point, four-color ballpoint pen or various colored fine-point pens (such as Micron pens) for writing in

your Bible. The Micron pens are best for this purpose. Office supply stores should have these.

3. Colored pencils or an eight-color Pentel pencil.

4. A composition notebook or loose-leaf notebook for working on your assignments and recording your insights.

SECOND

1. As you study this book, you'll find specific instructions for each day's study. The study should take you between 15 and 25 minutes a day. However, just know that the more time you can give to this study, the greater the spiritual dividends and the greater your intimacy with the Word of God and the God of the Word. If you are doing this study within the framework of a class and you find the lessons too heavy, simply do what you can. To do a little is better than to do nothing. Don't be an all-or-nothing person when it comes to Bible study.

As a word of warning, you need to be aware that any time you get into the Word of God, you enter into more intensive warfare with the devil (our enemy). Why? Every piece of the Christian's armor is related to the Word of God. And the enemy doesn't want you prepared for battle. Thus, the warfare! Remember that our one and only offensive weapon is the sword of the Spirit, which is the Word of God, and it is enough to fell the enemy.

To study or not to study is a matter of choice first, discipline second. It's a matter of the heart. On what or whom are you setting your heart? Get armed for war! And remember, victory is certain.

2. As you read each chapter, train yourself to think through the content of the text by asking the "5 W's and an H": who, what, when, where, why, and how. Posing questions like these and searching out the answers help you see

exactly what the Word of God is saying. When you interrogate the text with the 5 W's and an H, you ask questions like these:

a. **Who** are the main characters?

b. **What** is the chapter about?

c. **When** does this event or teaching take place?

d. **Where** does this occur?

e. **Why** is this being done or said?

f. **How** did this happen?

3. The "when" of events or teachings is very important and should be marked in an easily recognizable way in your Bible. We do this by putting a clock (like the one shown here) ⏰ in the margin of our Bibles beside the verse where the time phrase occurs. Or you may want to underline references to time in one specific color. As a reminder, note on your key-word bookmark (which is explained next in this section) how you are going to mark time references in each chapter.

4. You will be told about certain key words that you should mark throughout this study. This is the purpose of the colored pencils and the colored pen. While this may seem a little time-consuming, you will discover that it is a valuable learning tool. If you will develop the habit of marking your Bible, you will find it will make a significant difference in the effectiveness of your study and in how much you retain as a result of your study.

A **key word** is an important word that is used by the author repeatedly in order to convey his message to his reader. Certain key words will show up throughout the book, while other key words will be concentrated in specific chapters or segments of the book. When you mark a key word, you should also mark its synonyms (words that have the same meaning in a particular context) and any pronouns (*he, his, she, her, it, we, they, us, our, you, their, them*) in the same way you have marked the key word. Because some people have requested them, we will give you various ideas and suggestions in your daily assignments for how you can mark different key words.

Marking words for easy identification can be done by colors, symbols, or a combination of colors and symbols. However, colors are easier to distinguish than symbols. If you use symbols, we suggest you keep them very simple. For example, one of the key words in 1 Peter is *suffering*. You could draw a squiggle like flames of fire like this over suffering and color it orange. If a symbol is used in marking a key word, it is best for the symbol to somehow convey the meaning of the word.

As you begin this new venture, we recommend that you devise a color-coding system for marking key words that you decide to mark throughout your Bible. Then, when you glance at the pages of your Bible, you will have instant recognition of the words.

In marking the members of the Godhead (which we do not always mark), we use a triangle to represent the Father. We then color it yellow. Then, playing off the triangle, we mark the Son this way: Jesus , and the Holy Spirit this way: Spirit . We find that when you mark every reference to God and Jesus, your Bible becomes cluttered. However, since the Spirit is mentioned less and because many people do not have a thorough biblical understanding of the Holy Spirit, it is good to mark all the references to the Spirit of God.

When you start marking key words, it is easy to forget how you are marking them. Therefore, we recommend that you list the key words on an index card and use different symbols and/or colors to mark each word. Mark the words in the way you plan to mark each in the Bible text, and then use the card as a bookmark. Make one bookmark for words you are marking throughout your Bible, and a different one for any specific book of the Bible you are studying. Or record your marking system for the words you plan to mark throughout your Bible on a blank page in your Bible.

5. Because locations are important in Epistles and they tell you "where," you will find it helpful to mark geographical locations in a distinguishable way in your study. Try double underlining every reference to a location in green (grass and trees are green!). We suggest that you make a note on your key-word bookmark to mark locations.

6. Charts called 1 PETER AT A GLANCE, 2 PETER AT A GLANCE, and JUDE AT A GLANCE are located at the end of each section. When you complete your study of each chapter of these books, record the main theme of that chapter on the appropriate chart. A chapter theme is a brief description or summary of the main theme or predominant subject, teaching, or event covered in that chapter.

When stating chapter themes, it is best to use words found within the text itself and to be as brief as possible. Make sure that you do them in such a way as to distinguish one chapter from another. Doing this will help you to remember what each chapter is about. In addition, it will provide you with a ready reference if you desire to find something in the book rather quickly and without a lot of page-turning.

If you develop the habit of filling out the AT A GLANCE charts as you progress through the study, you will have a complete synopsis of the book when you finish. If you have a *New Inductive Study Bible*, you will find the same charts in your Bible. If you record your chapter themes on the charts in your Bible and on the designated line at the head of each chapter in the text, you'll always have a quick synopsis of the chapter and the book.

7. Begin your study with prayer. Don't start without it. Why? Well, although you are doing your part to handle the Word of God accurately, remember that the Bible is a divinely inspired book. The words you are reading are absolute truth, given to you by God so that you can know Him and His ways more intimately. These truths are divinely understood.

> For to us God revealed them through the Spirit;
> for the Spirit searches all things, even the depths
> of God. For who among men knows the thoughts
> of a man except the spirit of the man which is in
> him? Even so the thoughts of God no one knows
> except the Spirit of God (1 Corinthians 2:10,11).

This is why you need to pray. Simply tell God you want to understand His Word so you can live accordingly. Nothing pleases Him more than obedience—honoring Him as God—as you are about to see.

8. Each day, when you finish your lesson, take some time to think about what you read, what you saw with your own eyes. Ask your heavenly Father how you can apply these insights, principles, precepts, and commands to your own life. At times, depending on how God speaks to you through His Word, you might want to record these "Lessons for Life" in the margin of your Bible next to the text you have studied. Simply put "LFL" in the margin of

your Bible, then, as briefly as possible, record the lesson for life that you want to remember. You can also make the note "LFL" on your key word bookmark as a reminder to look for these when you study. You will find them encouraging (and sometimes convicting) when you come across them again. They will be a reminder of what God has shown you from His Word.

THIRD

This study is designed so that you have an assignment for every day of the week. This puts you where you should be—in the Word of God on a daily basis, grasping, systematizing, and utilizing truth. It's revolutionary!

If you will do your study daily, you will find it more profitable than doing a week's study in one sitting. Pacing yourself this way allows time for thinking through what you learn on a daily basis. However, whatever it takes to get it done, do it!

The seventh day of each week has several features that differ from the other six days. These features are designed to aid in one-on-one discipleship, group discussions, and Sunday school classes. However, they are also profitable even if you are studying this book by yourself.

The "seventh" day is whatever day in the week you choose to think about and/or discuss your week's study. On this day, you will find a verse or two to memorize and thus STORE IN YOUR HEART. This will help you focus on a major truth or truths covered in your study that week.

To assist those using the material for discipleship, family devotions, or in a Sunday school class or a group Bible study, there are QUESTIONS FOR DISCUSSION OR INDIVIDUAL STUDY. Whatever your situation, seeking to answer these questions will help you reason through some key issues in the study.

If you are using the study in a group setting, make sure the answers given are supported from the Bible text itself. This practice will help ensure that you are handling the Word of God accurately. As you learn to see what the text says, you will find that the Bible explains itself.

Always examine your insights by carefully observing the text to see what it *says*. Then, before you decide what the passage of Scripture *means*, make sure you interpret it in the light of its context. Context is what goes with the text...the Scriptures preceding and following what is written. Scripture will never contradict Scripture. If a Scripture passage ever seems to contradict the rest of the Word of God, you can be certain that something is being taken out of context. If you come to a passage that is difficult to understand, reserve your interpretations for a time when you can study the passage in greater depth.

Your discussion time should cause you to see how to apply these truths to your own life. What are you now going to embrace as truth? How are you going to order your life? Are you going to not only know these truths but also live accordingly?

The purpose of a Thought for the Week is to help you apply what you've learned. We've done this for your edification. In this, a little of our theology will inevitably come to the surface; however, we don't ask that you always agree with us. Rather, think through what is said in light of the context of the Word of God. You can determine how valuable it is.

Remember, books in the New Inductive Study Series are survey courses. If you want to do a more in-depth study of a particular book of the Bible, we suggest you do a Precept Upon Precept Bible Study Course on that book. The Precept studies are awesome but require five hours of personal study a week.

1 PETER

STANDING FIRM IN
DIFFICULT TIMES

These are difficult times. Christians are being restricted more and more in how they can express their beliefs. Morality has plummeted to new lows. Divorce is rampant. Love and commitment have all been given new definitions. Crime is more violent than ever. Sensuality is the predominant selling tool in advertising. Pornography is prevalent on television and in the movies. Sexual promiscuity is the norm among the youth. We live in a world of materialism. We spend all our energies on achieving and all our resources on obtaining. Temptations to yield to the former lusts are at times overwhelming.

How can believers resist all these influences that tend to woo us away from following the example of Christ? How can we stand when so many are falling?

Peter gives us the answers.

In 1 Peter we have recorded what Peter, under the inspiration of the Holy Spirit, wrote to the believers who had been scattered abroad due to the intense persecution of their day. These were difficult days for them, and it looked as if it was going to get worse. Peter writes to encourage the believers to stand firm during these difficult times.

His message is relevant for us today. We too are facing some difficult situations in our own lives. We need to be encouraged. In 1 Peter we will receive that exhortation as well as some practical instructions on standing firm during difficult times. You may be surprised to discover what Peter uses to motivate believers to "hang in there."

Once you understand and apply the principles given in this book, beloved of God, you will be able to stand firm in difficult times.

WHAT HAPPENED?

When you believed in Jesus Christ and were "born again," you received eternal life! Should that salvation experience have any effect on your everyday life? How should that event affect your responses, your relationships, your resolve?

Let's see what Peter had to say about it.

DAY ONE

When you study a book of the Bible, it is advantageous to read through the book as many times as possible. The more you read it, the easier it will be to understand what the book is about. Begin today to familiarize yourself with the content of 1 Peter by reading the entire book in one sitting. As you read, mark every reference to the author in a distinctive way or color. *The New Inductive Study Bible* suggests, when studying an epistle, mark the author in blue. This gives consistency to your marking system. When you mark the author, don't forget to mark personal pronouns.

As you do this, watch for any statement as to the author's purpose in writing. When you see this, record the author's name and his purpose in the appropriate place on the 1 PETER AT A GLANCE chart on page 56.

When you finish, record what you learn about the author in your notebook.

DAY TWO

Read chapter 1 of 1 Peter. This time, mark every reference to the recipients, including the personal pronouns (*you, your*), in a distinctive way or color. *The New Inductive Study Bible* suggests you use the color orange.

What is your first impression of the recipients? Record your thoughts in your notebook.

Now, look at the map on page 17 to get a better visual understanding of the exact territories where "those who reside as aliens" were scattered.

DAY THREE

Now read chapter 1 again. This time analyze every reference to the recipients. If the reference answers any of the "5 W's and an H" questions—who, what, when, where, why, and how—record in your notebook what you learn about the recipients. At this point, don't record any of the instructions from the author. We'll deal with those later. Just record those things that are specific about the recipients. Your lists would begin something like this:

THE RECIPIENTS
1. reside as aliens (1:1)
2. are chosen (1:1)
3.

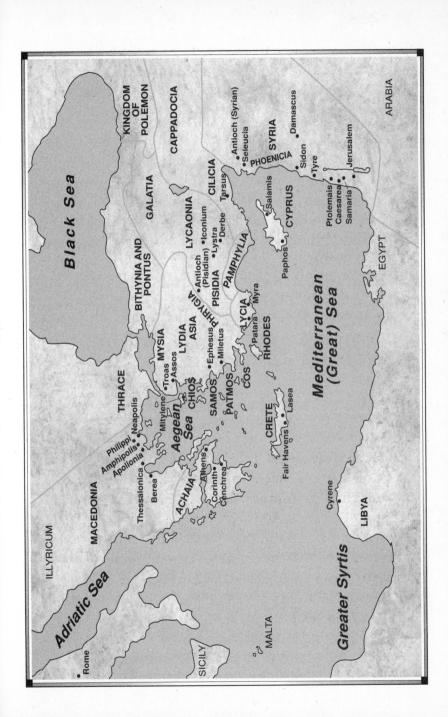

Put the chapter and verse next to each observation for future reference. Also, leave room in your notebook for other insights you'll discover about the recipients as you observe the remaining chapters of 1 Peter.

DAY FOUR

Read chapter 2 today, marking in your Bible and listing in your notebook your observations regarding the recipients. Don't forget to put the chapter and verse with each observation.

DAY FIVE

You guessed it! Chapter 3 is your assignment for today. Follow the same procedure as for yesterday.

DAY SIX

Finish the book of 1 Peter today by dealing with chapters 4 and 5 in the same way you did the previous chapters.

If you have time when you finish your assignment for today, prayerfully read down through your observations on the recipients and record in your notebook the major subjects Peter discusses in this letter.

DAY SEVEN

 Store in your heart: 1 Peter 1:3-5.
 Read and discuss: 1 Peter 1:1-16; 5:10-12.

QUESTIONS FOR DISCUSSION OR INDIVIDUAL STUDY

∽ Who is the author of this epistle? How does he describe himself?

∽ To whom is this letter written? What did you learn about them? Where are they? Why are they there? How are they described?

∽ What were the recipients going through at this time? How were they responding? What would they obtain as an outcome of their faith?

∽ How did the prophets serve the recipients? What did the prophets bring to them?

∽ Why did the author write to the recipients? Where is this purpose stated? How does what you learned about the recipients in 1 Peter relate to the purpose of the book?

∽ What subjects did Peter discuss? How do they relate to the purpose of the book? Were any of these subjects of special interest to you? Why?

∽ Are you going through any trials at this time? Are you standing firm?

∽ Does your life in any way parallel the recipients in 1 Peter? How?

∽ What did you learn as a result of your study this week? Did any insight you recorded speak to you in a personal way?

THOUGHT FOR THE WEEK

Our focus this week has been on the recipients of 1 Peter. They did not live in an ideal situation or in perfect circumstances. To the contrary, they were going through various trials that resulted in much suffering. It almost sounds like a current report on the Christian life today— anxious situations, false accusations, slanderous remarks, intimidation, unfair treatment, and harsh bosses. Because believers live "in" the world but are not part "of" the world, they are like aliens and strangers. They are in constant conflict with those who reside on planet Earth but have not yet experienced "the true grace of God." Because this is true, there will always be tension between believers and unbelievers.

Peter encouraged them to stand firm regardless of the circumstances. They could only do this by His grace and their obedience. Although those who had been scattered abroad had experienced the grace of God, they needed to be reminded of exactly what that grace was and how it affected their everyday lives. They also needed to be reminded of what they were to *do* and *not do* in response to all the abrasive situations they were in so they could maintain their testimony in the community and bring glory to God in all their relationships.

God showed them where they were spiritually, who they were in Christ, what was going on in their lives, what was going to come their way, and how they were to respond. Everything they needed for whatever they were told to do, He had already provided for them by His grace! And the same is true for you. What a life! In need of everything but lacking nothing! His provision—grace and peace—is always in the fullest measure! May you experience the same, beloved.

STAND FIRM IN HIS GRACE

∾∾∾∾

Since you became a believer, do you ever find yourself going through difficult times? How do you respond to these circumstances? Does your response to these uncontrollable, unwanted, unexpected trials have an effect on your relationship with God and with others?

How then does Peter say you should respond, and on what does he base his advice?

DAY ONE

As you saw last week, Peter wrote to the scattered aliens "exhorting and testifying that this is the true grace of God" and then urged them to stand firm in it—in that grace. Read chapter 1 of 1 Peter and mark every reference to *salvation* (also *born again*[1]), *grace*, and *faith* (*believe, believers*), each in their own distinctive way. If you want to follow the suggestions in the NISB, color grace blue and put a yellow border around it. Mark faith like this faith in purple with the inside shaded green.

DAY TWO

Today, read through chapter 1 once more and record in your notebook what you learn about *grace, salvation,* and *faith.* As you do this assignment, notice how these three subjects interrelate. Also, as you record your observations about *salvation,* you may learn some truths about this subject in verses where neither the word *salvation* nor the words *born again* appear, but the concept of salvation is being discussed. Do this prayerfully, and it will help you see everything that Peter has to say on this subject in chapter 1.

DAY THREE

Read 1 Peter 1. First, look for and mark the synonyms used to express the suffering of the recipients: *distressed*[2] *by various trials* and *tested*[3] *by fire.* Also mark the key words *rejoice* (*joy*) and *glory* (*glories*), each in its own distinctive way.

List what you learn about *trials* and *tests* in your notebook under the heading SUFFERINGS, and allow space for truths you will learn in the following chapters about this subject. Also record your observations about *rejoice* and *glory.*

Analyze the relationship between these three key words or subjects. Write out your conclusion. Pause here to evaluate how you respond to the various trials that come into your life. Do you respond as the recipients did? What enabled them to respond in this way? What did this response produce?

DAY FOUR

Now read chapter 1 once more. This time, mark every reference to God, Jesus, and the Holy Spirit, each in its own distinctive way. Be sure to include any synonyms or pronouns. The *NISB* suggests the following symbols:

As you mark these, list in your notebook what you learn about each person of the trinity and what has happened through them.

DAY FIVE

An instruction is a command to *do* something. Read 1 Peter 1:13-25 and record in your notebook Peter's instructions to the recipients.

Analyze how these instructions relate to the purpose statement found in chapter 5.

Look again at 1 Peter 1:13. This verse begins with the word "Therefore." This is a term of conclusion or result. In other words, a conclusion is being drawn or a result is being indicated. Review what you learned from the first 12 verses, and determine what conclusion is being made or what result is being shown in these last verses of this chapter.

Evaluate these instructions in light of your own walk with the Lord. Are you doing these things in your daily walk with Him? If not, you may want to pause right here and spend a few moments asking God to help you incorporate these principles into your life. Just by doing this study you are already working on the first instruction.

DAY SIX

It doesn't seem like this is the final day of this week's study. This chapter has been so encouraging! I pray that you have been learning about the true grace of God and are being strengthened daily to stand firm in the grace brought to you in your salvation.

Today, begin your study by reading verses 10-12 of chapter 1. As you read these verses, record what you learn about the prophets. Be sure to observe their role in the recipient's salvation.

Now read verses 13-21 and mark every use of *holy* using a purple cloud shaded in yellow ⌒⌒ as the *NISB* suggests. Note the contrast Peter uses in these verses to make his point.

Read verses 22-25 of chapter 1. As you read these verses, mark every reference to the *Word of God*. When you've completed the markings, record what you learn about the Word of God in your notebook. Don't miss one detail—it is rich!

One final assignment for today and you will complete your study of chapter 1. Read chapter 1 again. As you do, mark in a distinctive way all the references to *time, times,* and related phrases. The *NISB* suggests a green clock ⏰ . As you do this assignment, note the connection between some of these "time" phrases and the subject of salvation.

Having completed your study of chapter 1, record the main theme of this chapter on the 1 PETER AT A GLANCE chart on page 56.

DAY SEVEN

 Store in your heart: 1 Peter 1:18,19.
Read and discuss: 1 Peter 1.

QUESTIONS FOR DISCUSSION OR INDIVIDUAL STUDY

∾ What did you learn about salvation? How do grace and faith interrelate with salvation?

∞ If you wanted to use 1 Peter 1 to explain salvation to someone, how would you describe the roles of God the Father, Jesus Christ, and the Holy Spirit?

∞ What did you learn about the Word of God? What role does the Word of God play in salvation?

∞ What role did the prophets play in the salvation of the recipients?

∞ What were the recipients' circumstances? How were they responding to their circumstances? What made that response possible? What was the result of their response? How do you respond to trials?

∞ What benefits did the recipients possess as a result of their salvation? What were they looking forward to?

∞ What "time" phrases were mentioned? How do those phrases relate to salvation?

∞ What instructions did Peter give to the recipients? How do these instructions relate to the purpose statement of the book? How do these instructions relate to your daily walk with the Lord? Are there any areas of weakness? What do you intend to do to resolve those conflicts between what the Word of God says you are to do and what you are doing?

∞ What conclusion is being drawn in verse 13? Relate verses 1-12 to verses 13-25.

∞ What did you learn about the key word *holy*? What contrast did Peter make in verses 13-21 to make his point? How would you describe the recipients' former lifestyle?

❧ How does the author begin to fulfill his purpose statement in chapter 1? How did he exhort the recipients? What testimony of the true grace of God did he give? What instructions did he give them to help them stand firm in that grace regardless of their circumstances?

❧ What is the main theme of chapter 1?

THOUGHT FOR THE WEEK

Peter begins this epistle to believers scattered abroad and living as aliens by telling them what God did for them in salvation. Then, after painting the awesome picture of redemption, he moves to what they are to do in order to stand firm. Preparing their minds for action, keeping sober in spirit, and fixing their hope on the grace that was to come at the revelation of Jesus would allow them to live as obedient children, holy in all their behavior and not conformed to their former lusts. They were to conduct themselves in fear while residing as aliens on this earth, realizing that their citizenship was in heaven and they were just passing through. But while here, it would be important for them to fervently love the brethren from their heart because their souls had been purified by the truth.

Everything Peter tells them to do is based on what God, through salvation, has done for them. For instance, how in the world could they ever be holy if the Holy Spirit had not set them apart for divine service and the blood of Jesus had not cleansed them from all their sins? God chose them, set them apart, redeemed them, cleansed them, forgave them, empowered them, and promised them an eternal inheritance that would not perish, be defiled, or fade away, but would be forever reserved in heaven for them. They didn't deserve it. They had not earned it. God just did it on the basis of His grace—His unmerited favor.

Surely those who had been scattered abroad were encouraged after being reminded of all that God had done for them through His grace. Because of that grace, they could stand the fires of testing and still give praise, glory, and honor to the Lord. That grace would enable them to resist the temptations of the former lusts and be holy. It would enable them to fervently love one another from the heart regardless of how they were treated.

Now let me ask you some very important questions, questions that once considered and answered will solidify your position with God. Has He chosen you? Set you apart? Redeemed you with His blood? Forgiven you of your personal sins? Have you obeyed His call by responding in faith to believe in His Son? Have you been born again? If so, you have an inheritance reserved in heaven! If not, you can trust in Him now! Go back and read through your observations on salvation and simply follow the instructions given in those verses. Believe!

It has been our prayer that you have been encouraged by what you have learned about the true grace of God. As a believer, you can trust Him in your daily trials, temptations, and relationships. He has a wonderful inheritance to give you when He returns again. You will be delivered from the presence of sin, temptation, and suffering forever. What a marvelous salvation! What marvelous grace! Stand firm in it.

ACTING LIKE SAINTS

There is an old saying, "Quit acting like a baby and start acting like a man!" This saying is based on four statements:

I once was a baby.

Because I once was a baby, I know how to act like a baby.

I am a man.

Because I am a man, I know how to act like a man.

I heard a preacher draw a parallel with that old saying by saying this: "Quit acting like a sinner and start acting like a saint." This, too, is based on four statements:

I once was a sinner.

Because I once was a sinner, I know how to act like a sinner.

I am a saint.

Because I am a saint, I know how to act like a saint.

Can a saint act like a sinner? Can a sinner act like a saint? Can you tell the difference? If so, how?

DAY ONE

The chapter and verse divisions in the Bible are man-made. You cannot assume that each time you come to another chapter in the Bible, you come to another subject. As you begin this week's study, read 1 Peter 1:22–2:3. Mark the key words *word*[4] and *salvation*[5] the same way you did last week and add your new insights to those lists in your notebook. Also, add to your list the instruction given in 1 Peter 2:1-3.

You probably noticed that chapter 2 begins with "Therefore[6]," a term of conclusion. Read 1 Peter 1:22–2:3 once again and, in your notebook, write out what is being concluded and on what basis.

Sometimes the words used in Scripture are not words we use in our daily conversation. Therefore we don't always understand what is being said. Look at the brief definitions below and then reread 1 Peter 2:1-3, inserting them in the appropriate place for a better understanding of this passage.

malice	vicious character
deceit[7]	craftiness, treachery
hypocrisy	pretense, insincerity
envy	displeasure at seeing the prosperity of others
slander[8]	speaking evil of someone

Now to complete your assignment for today, review the things that the recipients were to "put aside" and prayerfully ask yourself if any of those things on occasion have crept into your life. If so, what should you do when you recognize these behaviors, and what effect will putting them aside have on your desire for the Word of God?

DAY TWO

Today, read all of chapter 2. As you do, mark every reference to *Jesus* and *God* including synonyms and pronouns for both. Mark them as you did in chapter 1.

Now read the chapter again, adding to your list everything you learn about God.

DAY THREE

As you read 1 Peter 2 today, add any new insights you glean about Jesus to the list in your notebook.

DAY FOUR

Read through the entire chapter again today and mark the following key words in the same distinct way you did in chapter 1, adding any insights to the appropriate lists: *believe(s)*[9], *word*[10] (you've already marked this in verse 2), *holy, glorify,* and any phrases that have to do with *time.*

There are several new subjects introduced in chapter 2 that did not appear in chapter 1. Read through chapter 2 and mark distinctively every reference to the *behavior* of the recipients. You will recognize this subject by the use of phrases such as *good deeds*[11], *do right*[12], *doing right,* and *doing what is right*[13].

DAY FIVE

You've already added to your list from verse 2 the first instruction in chapter 2. Read through the chapter and add the other instructions to your list, reflecting on how these instructions relate to the purpose statement.

Also, consider how these instructions relate to your personal behavior.

In the remaining time you have today, read verses 18-25 and mark the key word *suffering*[14] (also mark in the same way *sufferings, suffered,* and *harshly treated*). Add to your list from chapter 1 what you learn about suffering from these verses.

DAY SIX

Your final day this week will be spent looking at the other new subject introduced this week. First, read verses 11-20 and mark the word *submit.*

Read verses 11-17 and record in your notebook your observations regarding who the recipients were to submit to and for what purpose. Also note the result this behavior would bring.

Now read verses 18-20, marking the word *submissive*[15] in the same way and answer the same questions for this passage as you did in the previous verses.

Does submission interrelate with behavior and suffering? If so, how?

Review all your work from this week and record the main theme of this chapter on the 1 PETER AT A GLANCE chart.

DAY SEVEN

 Store in your heart: 1 Peter 2:9.
Read and discuss: 1 Peter 1:22–2:25.

QUESTIONS FOR DISCUSSION OR INDIVIDUAL STUDY

- ∾ What conclusion is Peter drawing in 2:1 with his "Therefore"? What had he just finished saying about the Word of God? Because of that truth, what does he want them to do in the future? What things are they to put out of their life? Do you have any of these things in your life now? Will these things affect your desire for the Word of God? What is essential for growing in your salvation?

- ∾ As far as their relationship with the Word of God, what is the difference between the recipients in 1:22 and those described in 2:8? Does it make a difference how you respond to the Word of God?

- ∾ What did you learn about Jesus this week? What did He do for you? What is His example?

- ∾ What truths did you observe about God?

- ∾ What "time" phrase did you see in chapter 2? How does this phrase relate to the "time" phrases in chapter 1?

- ∾ What were the instructions in this chapter? How do these relate to the purpose statement? How do the instructions relate to the behavior of the recipients? Why is behavior so important to nonbelievers?

- ∾ How were the recipients to respond to slander and harsh treatment? Why? What would be the result?

∾ What did you learn about submission? How does submission to authorities and masters show in whom you are putting your trust? How does the relationship between servants and masters relate to your workplace today? How do you find favor with your boss? With God?

∾ What did you learn this week from your personal study of this chapter? Which instruction had the most impact on you personally? Is your behavior in line with what you've learned this week?

THOUGHT FOR THE WEEK

In chapter 2, Peter discusses two new concepts: submission and doing what is right. He also gives us several new portraits of Jesus—a living stone, the cornerstone, an example, a suffering Savior, the Shepherd and Guardian of our souls. Obviously, these relate to each other. How does all this information relate to us, in our situations, in our circumstances, in our daily lives? What is God saying to us?

The study this week has caused us to reflect on what God has done for us through the life, death, and resurrection of Jesus. This gives us the opportunity to die to sin, to live to righteousness, and to respond in a more Christlike way to those who treat us harshly or cause us to suffer unjustly.

We may sometimes receive harsh treatment because we have done something wrong and we deserve that kind of a response. Sometimes, however, we do what is right and unjustly receive harsh treatment. Peter wanted his readers to know what our response should be when we are abused and no fault can be found in us. It's a matter of trusting that God is still in charge even though it seems that things are out of control. He will judge fairly and righteously.

In verse 19 the word "favor" is the same word that is translated "grace" in other places. It's the English transliteration of the Greek word *charis*.* This word means "unmerited, undeserved, or unexpected favor." Peter has gone to great lengths to show the unmerited, undeserved, unexpected favor that God has shown to those who believe in His Son, Jesus. Peter is saying that a slave who suffers under an unreasonable master should be submissive to his master because this finds favor (grace) with God. Why? An unreasonable master would not expect his abused slave to respond with submission and respect. When he does, the unreasonable master is then the recipient of the slave's grace. Why should the slave respond this way? His submission gives him a clear conscience toward God, and it finds favor with God. What the slave has received, the slave can give. What the slave gives, the slave receives!

Now that we know a little more about what God has done for us through Jesus, we are better prepared to respond in a Christlike manner to those difficult tyrants that malign and mistreat us. Our reactions may not yet always be what they should be, but we have more information now to help us make the right choices so we won't be ruled by our emotions.

We are indeed a chosen race, a royal priesthood, a holy nation, and a people for God's own possession. We no longer live in darkness. We now live in His marvelous light and can proclaim His excellencies not only with our lips but also with our lives. We must continually choose to keep entrusting ourselves to Him who judges righteously as we follow the example that has been set before us. We can act like saints—that is who we are!

---

* A transliteration substitutes the letters of one alphabet for another. In this case, each English letter replaces a Greek letter. Every time we refer to a Greek word in this book, we use its English transliteration.

LOVING LIFE AND SEEING GOOD DAYS

Do you wake up each day excited about life? Is every day a good day? You might answer, "If it weren't for people, I would enjoy life. I would have a good day every day! It's the people who mess up my life and ruin my days." Then, my friend, I have a question for you: Is it possible to love life and see good days regardless of what others say about you or what others do to you? Let's see what Peter said about that.

DAY ONE

This week will be spent studying chapter 3. Remember, this study is not designed to plumb the depths of every verse or phrase, but rather to get you acquainted with 1 Peter so that you have a good general overview of the book. Therefore, begin your personal study time today by prayerfully reading the entire chapter, marking all the key words as in previous chapters. Of course, add any new insights to the appropriate lists.

DAY TWO

When Peter says, "In the same way"[16] in verses 1 and 7, to what "same way" is he referring? Briefly review the work you did in chapter 2 regarding this subject to see the context of that phrase.

Now read verses 1-7 and examine them in light of the 5 W's and an H. Then, in your notebook, make a chart with two headings: WIVES and HUSBANDS. List all you learn about the wives today. We'll do the husbands tomorrow.

DAY THREE

Read 1 Peter 3:1-7 once again. Be sure to interrogate the text carefully, listing all you learn about the husbands on your notebook chart.

Read those first seven verses once again, and add the instructions Peter gives to the wives and to the husbands to that ongoing list in your notebook.

DAY FOUR

Read verses 8-17 and add the instructions to your list.

Go back through these verses once again and mark in a distinctive way the word *evil*. List in your notebook what you learn, including the consequences of choosing this type of behavior.

DAY FIVE

Today, read 1 Peter 3:8-17. You marked *behavior* (and all its synonyms) as well as *suffer* on Day One of this week. Evaluate how these interrelate with evil and the instructions given in this section. Write out your conclusions. As you do this, be sure to determine from the text the current circumstances of the recipients and how this relates to this passage. Also, consider the impact these conclusions should have on the believer's life.

DAY SIX

Read 1 Peter 3:14-22 today asking the 5 W's and an H. Go slowly. This is your only assignment for today, so you'll have plenty of time. Add to your JESUS list in your notebook the truths you learn about Him from these verses. Relate these truths to your SALVATION list.

Review your work and record the main theme of chapter 3 on the 1 PETER AT A GLANCE chart.

DAY SEVEN

Store in your heart: 1 Peter 3:14-17.
Read and discuss: 1 Peter 3.

QUESTIONS FOR DISCUSSION OR INDIVIDUAL STUDY

∞ Discuss what you learned this week about wives and husbands. Were the husbands referred to in verse 1 believers or unbelievers? Why do you say that? Can you support your view with scripture from 1 Peter?

∞ According to 1 Peter 3:3,4, are women forbidden to wear jewelry? Braid their hair? Wear dresses? What is the focus of these verses? What should a woman focus on? What does her behavior have to do with the salvation of her nonbelieving husband?

∞ If you are married, how would you evaluate yourself in light of the instructions Peter gives to wives and husbands? If you are a wife, do you submit to your husband, even if he is not a believer? Should you obey him if he tells you to do something that violates what the Bible clearly teaches? If you are a husband, do you treat your wife in an understanding way? Do you honor your wife as a fellow heir of the grace of life? Are your prayers being hindered in any way? If your prayers are being hindered, where should you check first?

∾ What five attitudes should believers have?

∾ What is your normal reaction to someone who treats you with evil or insults you?

∾ What should your reaction be according to what you learned this week?

∾ How are believers to behave when nonbelievers inflict suffering on them? What happens when believers behave this way? What circumstances were the recipients of 1 Peter living in? How do Peter's instructions relate to these circumstances?

∾ What did you learn about Jesus from chapter 3? According to this chapter, what did God do for believers through Jesus?

THOUGHT FOR THE WEEK

Christ voluntarily submitted to the Father's will and bore our sins in His body on the cross—the just for the unjust. He committed no sin, nor was any deceit found in His mouth. *He was guilty only of doing what was right.*

We have an example to follow in every relationship. That example is Jesus. We live with others in this world. No matter what the relationships are—government ruler to citizen, employer to employee, husband to wife, wife to husband, believer to believer, saved to the lost—the ideal would be that all could live together and be of one mind. That we could live together like brothers with true love and sympathy for each other, compassionate and humble, even speaking well of those who mistreat and malign. This is not life as we know it today. Most people do what is right *in their own eyes.*

Jesus gave us the pattern of how to do what is right *in His Father's eyes.*

> He submitted to the Father's will,
>   and even though He suffered,
>   He patiently endured it all.
>
> He continually kept entrusting Himself and His
>   situation to God,
>   and even though it took a terminal turn,
>   God brought life out of a lifeless situation.

My friend, no matter how impossible your situation seems, no matter how bad the relationship is, follow in His steps. Submit and do what is right, even if you know you will suffer for it. God will give you whatever you need to endure. Keep constantly, continually, consistently entrusting yourself and your situation to Him, remembering that at times it will look like there is no justice in what is going on, no truth in what is being said, or no life left in the situation. But remember that God, the righteous Judge, has the final word, and He is able to bring life out of death, to His praise and glory and honor.

You have been called for this purpose. You have been encouraged, even commanded by Peter to follow in the steps of Jesus. Now you know the steps. You can no longer return to the former lusts of your ignorance. Now you must follow Him or walk in disobedience to the Word. When you put your foot in His footprint, then and only then will you love life and see good days regardless of what others do to you!

No Turning Back

~~~~~

Not everyone is happy that you became a Christian. Some cannot believe that you will no longer "hang out" with them. Some will malign you because of your decision.

What will keep you motivated to continue to live in intimacy with Him even during difficult times of persecution?

DAY ONE

Read chapter 4 today, marking all the key words as in previous chapters. As you move through the chapter, remember to ask the 5 W's and an H of the text so this doesn't become a mechanical marking exercise.

DAY TWO

There is a repeated phrase used at the end of chapter 3 and in the beginning of chapter 4 that Peter has not used so far in this book. Read 1 Peter 3:18–4:6 and mark distinctively the repeated phrase *in the flesh*.[17] As you mark this phrase, make a list of the truths you learn from these verses in your notebook.

You probably noticed in these opening verses of chapter 4 the repetition of another phrase, *the will of God*.[18] Underline that phrase in these opening verses, but continue to read the rest of this chapter for one other mention of this phrase. Record what you learn about the will of God in your notebook.

DAY THREE

Now focus again on the first 6 verses of this chapter. Read these verses and record in your notebook what you learn about the Gentiles. Relate these truths about the Gentiles to the recipients. Consider what happened to the recipients that brought about this drastic change in their behavior and in the way their former friends treated them.

DAY FOUR

There are some key words that are distinctive to this chapter. Read through the entire chapter today marking *judge* (and its synonyms), *gospel*, and *rejoice*. Also, while doing this make sure that you have marked the references to time just like you've done previously.

Record in your notebook what you've learned about the judgment of God.

DAY FIVE

Read 1 Peter 4 today, asking the who, what, when, where, why, and how questions, adding the instructions to your ongoing list in your notebook. As you record these observations, evaluate how these instructions relate to you in your present daily life.

Once again, read through this chapter, analyzing how suffering and glory interrelate.

DAY SIX

Your final assignment for this week is to read through the chapter and mark every reference to the trinity: *God, Jesus,* and *the Holy Spirit.* Record in your notebook what you learn about each as well as what has been done through them.

Consider all your work in this chapter, reviewing your notes, and record the chapter theme on the 1 PETER AT A GLANCE chart.

DAY SEVEN

Store in your heart: 1 Peter 4:19.
Read and discuss: 1 Peter 4.

QUESTIONS FOR DISCUSSION OR INDIVIDUAL STUDY

∞ What did you learn about the phrase "in the flesh"? According to 1 Peter 3:18-19, what did Jesus do when He died for our sins? Discuss the relationship between our salvation experience and the life we are to live "the rest of the time in the flesh."

∞ What description is given of "the desire of the Gentiles"? How did the nonbelieving Gentiles respond to the recipients' salvation? How does this response relate to the recipients' circumstances? What role will God play in this?

❧ What instructions did Peter give the recipients in this chapter? How do these instructions relate to their suffering? What will be the end result if they obey these commands? What is to be their response while going through their fiery ordeal?

❧ What did you learn about God's judgment? Where will it begin?

❧ Discuss what you learned about the will of God. How does the will of God relate to suffering?

❧ To whom are the "special gifts" given? What two kinds of gifts are mentioned? What are the recipients of these gifts to do with them?

❧ Can someone suffer and be in the will of God? What should they do when going through a fiery ordeal according to the will of God? How do they do that, practically speaking?

THOUGHT FOR THE WEEK

Thus far Peter has eloquently expounded on the marvelous and true grace of God. He has taken a heavenly brush and dipped it into redemptive colors, painting for us a magnificently beautiful portrait of God's grace.

We are benefactors of what God has done for us through His abundant provision. Each of us is important. Each of us is necessary. Each of us is significant. He has gifted each of us with supernatural abilities through the power of His Spirit. He has provided each of us with opportunities—responsibilities of ministry that are compatible with our gifts—and He brings about the effects He desires.

However, we still live in the flesh. Our society is dominated by the lusts of men. The world in which we live pays little or no attention to biblical moral standards. Sometimes the world reacts violently against the standard of God's righteousness. Who would have ever thought that individuals would be punished for doing what is right?

We are motivated to patiently endure when we gaze at the portrait of grace. However, the persistent calling back to a former lifestyle is distracting at times. Maybe that's why Peter, at this point in the letter, reminds us of the will and judgment of God.

Peter reminds us that even in light of all that God has done for us, it is His will for us, on occasion, to suffer for doing what is right rather than avoiding suffering by doing what is called right by the standards of men. It is the will of God for our lifestyles to be according to His plan rather than the pleasurable schemes of men.

And even though He bore our sins in His own body on the cross, in the future we will stand before Him while He impartially judges our works accomplished on planet Earth. He is ready to judge righteously. He begins with us, the household of God.

What a balance—the grace of God and the judgment of God. You are the recipient of the unmerited favor of God. Live in the light of it because you are accountable. Keep your eyes on the portrait of His grace!

The Blessing of Suffering

Have you ever wondered why bad things happen to really good people? Have you ever gone through a time of difficulty and pain when, as far as you knew, you were doing what was right, when you weren't doing anything wrong?

Have you ever felt that, to the best of your knowledge and ability, you were in the perfect center of the will of God when all of a sudden, it happened—a tragedy, a catastrophe?

The biblical teaching is clear: no one is exempt from attending the schoolhouse of suffering. Suffering is a part of the Christian life. It cannot be avoided. God allows suffering to happen to those who are His. However, the question has to be asked: What should be accomplished in the life of the believer when he/she goes through a time of suffering?

You'll find your answers in this week's study of 1 Peter 5.

DAY ONE

This is the final week of our study of the book of 1 Peter. You have learned so much in the last five weeks!

But then again, there's still so much to learn about this book. You almost have a complete overview of 1 Peter.

Your assignment today is to read through the entire text of chapter 5 and mark the key words. Ask the who, what, where, when, why, and how questions as you read through this chapter. Try to discern what subjects are being talked about. Add any new insights you learn to your ongoing lists for the key words.

DAY TWO

Read 1 Peter 5 again today. This time, list every instruction that Peter gives to his readers in your notebook along with the others from previous chapters.

DAY THREE

Today, begin your time with the Lord in prayer, asking Him to illuminate for you the truths that are in this chapter that you may gain insight into His will for your life.

Now read verses 1-5 and record in your notebook your insights about the elders and the younger men. Analyze not only what they were to do but also how they were to do it.

Now read verses 5-7 marking *humble* in a distinctive way. Make a list of what you learn in your notebook. Notice whom Peter is now addressing.

DAY FOUR

Today evaluate verses 8 and 9 by observing what you learn about the devil. Record your observations in your notebook.

Now read through chapter 5, pausing at each reference to suffering and listing who it is that is suffering. Prayerfully look at this and consider whose company you keep when you go through difficult times for your faith.

Your final assignment for today is to read through this chapter and list the things God will do for you. As you are doing this, make sure to note your responsibility in each of these demonstrations of the grace of God.

Record the chapter theme for chapter 5 on the 1 PETER AT A GLANCE chart.

DAY FIVE

Today, you could be tempted to skip over your assignment or take it lightly. Go back and prayerfully read chapters 1 and 2 of 1 Peter. As you read them again, take in the message as if this epistle were written to you personally. Let this letter be your prayer. You may even want to substitute your name in place of the recipients'. Grasp what God has done for you through His grace. This is the true grace of God! Also, review what you should be doing in order to stand firm in that grace regardless of your circumstances. Ask God to make this message applicable and practical to you today. Ask Him to reveal to you any changes or adjustments that you need to make in order to bring your life into full compliance with what He's revealed to you in your study of 1 Peter.

DAY SIX

Today, prayerfully read chapters 3, 4, and 5 the same way you read chapters 1 and 2 yesterday. Once again, let me encourage you to approach this assignment prayerfully. God may show you some truths that you didn't see as you went through these chapters the first time.

Now, your final assignment for today is to put the capstone in place. What is the book of 1 Peter about? Record the book theme on the 1 PETER AT A GLANCE chart. Also, fill in any information requested on the chart that you have not yet recorded.

DAY SEVEN

Store in your heart: 1 Peter 5:10.
Read and discuss: 1 Peter 5.

QUESTIONS FOR DISCUSSION OR INDIVIDUAL STUDY

∞ What did Peter exhort the elders to do? How were they to do it? What insights do you gain about their circumstances from these exhortations to the elders?

∞ What did he tell the younger men to do? What reason did Peter give them for subjecting themselves to the elders?

∞ Whom is Peter addressing in the beginning of verse 5? At the end?

∞ What instructions did Peter give the recipients in chapter 5? What did you learn about humility? What did you learn about the devil? How do the three of these relate to each other?

∞ What new truths did you learn about the true grace of God in this chapter?

∾ What have you learned from 1 Peter about the true grace of God? What have you learned about standing firm in the true grace of God?

∾ According to chapter 5, who suffered? Is anyone exempt from suffering? What will God do for them after they had suffered for a little while?

∾ What have you learned from the entire book of 1 Peter about suffering? About what your behavior should be? About submission? About salvation? About the importance of the Word of God?

∾ How do your chapter themes for 1 Peter relate to the purpose of the book? How do they relate to your book theme for 1 Peter?

∾ How has God spoken to you personally through this study? What is the most significant thing you learned? What surprised you the most in this book?

THOUGHT FOR THE WEEK

It was once said that suffering is the school that God sends His children through so that He might teach them how to trust Him.

Suffering is inevitable for the believer. None is exempt. Suffering crosses all social, financial, physical, cultural, and political strata. The popular suffer and the prominent suffer. The prosperous suffer and the powerful suffer. The poor suffer and even the pious suffer. Suffering is impartial, unbiased. It has no conscience. It goes where it desires, it goes where it is sent. It goes where it is unwelcome, it goes where it is unwanted. Suffering has no timing. Sometimes it's brief, sometimes it lingers. Sometimes it just stays...and stays...and stays. Suffering is certain...but God has the final word!

Look at what God tells us in 1 Peter:

- ∞ Even though you may be distressed for a little while by various trials, you are protected by the power of God through your faith, and in this you will greatly rejoice (1:6).

- ∞ The proof of your faith will result in praise and glory and honor at the revelation of Jesus Christ (1:7).

- ∞ When you bear up under the sorrow of unjust suffering, you find favor with Him (2:19).

- ∞ When you patiently endure suffering for having done what is right, you find favor with Him (2:20).

- ∞ You have been called for the purpose of suffering just like Jesus, our example (2:21).

- ∞ You are to keep entrusting yourself to Him while suffering (2:23).

- ∞ Even if you suffer for the sake of righteousness, you are blessed (3:14).

- ∞ It is better that you suffer for doing what is right than for doing what is wrong (3:17).

- ∞ You are not to be surprised at the fiery ordeals among you, which come upon you for your testing (4:12).

- ∞ You are to share in the sufferings of Christ and keep on rejoicing so that at the revelation of His glory, you may rejoice with exultation (4:13).

- ∞ You are not to be ashamed when you suffer, but in the name of Christ glorify God (4:16).

- ∾ When you suffer according to the will of God, you are to entrust your souls to a faithful Creator in doing what is right (4:19).

- ∾ Christ suffered (5:1).

- ∾ Your brethren who are in the world are suffering (5:9).

- ∾ You will suffer (5:10).

- ∾ But God will perfect you, confirm you, strengthen you, and establish you because He is the God of all grace and He has called you for this purpose (5:10).

This is the true grace of God. Stand firm in it. Glory awaits you.

Theme of 1 Peter: Christian Hope

	SEGMENT DIVISIONS	CHAPTER THEMES
Author: Peter		
Historical Setting:		1 Salvation, Dedication, & Sanctification
		2
Purpose:		
		3
Key Words:		4
		5

2 PETER

Kept Safe by the Truth

My family loves to decorate for Christmas. It's their favorite time of the year. One of my jobs is to decorate the outside of the house with lights. Trimming the outline of the roof from the top of a ladder is fairly easy—not much of a challenge really. Trimming the second-story dormer windows is a totally different story. The pitch or angle of the roof is steep, and my tendency is to slide down. Obviously, I don't want to slide down because there is a point where sliding *down* the roof becomes sliding *off* the roof. The solution is to find something to hold me in place, something to keep me from falling. I run a safety line or rope over the top of the house, tying it off to a strong tree on the side of the house opposite the dormers. I then climb the ladder to the roof and tie the line around myself. The result is (that I look silly and) that I have a safety line to hold me in place. Two things are really important at this point. First, that the safety line is strong enough to hold me, and second, that I actually use it. If it is too weak to hold me, it is not really a safety line. If I don't connect myself to it, I am not really safe. As long as I am attached to a safety line—a real safety line—I am safe from falling; I am held in place.

We need a spiritual safety line. We need a cord of absolute truth to keep us from sliding down a slippery slope of error and off into absolute nonsense. The Word of God is that safety line. The Word of God is the only safety line. It is truth—absolute truth—and it is strong enough to hold me. Peter, in his second letter, is offering a safety line to people who are in danger of believing a lie. They are being confronted with false teachers and deceptive error. They have questions about the truth and how they should live. Questions that Peter answers in a clear, straightforward manner.

We are in the same position today. We are confronted with the same type of teachers and the same issues. We are even told it doesn't matter what we use as a safety line, as long as we *believe* it will hold us. But it does matter. Truth is truth, error is not. The Bible is the safety line. Will you connect yourself to it and be held firmly in place?

In this study we will see how to live with discernment in the end times, how to be held in place by the truth, how to be kept from falling.

LIVING BY
KNOWING THE TRUTH

Our safety line is the truth. Are you secure? This week we will begin to understand this letter and by the end of this five-week study, if you persevere, you will be secure in the truth.

If you want to live with discernment, this study is for you, my friend.

DAY ONE

The first step in our study will be to become familiar with 2 Peter. We want you to get a feel for the letter, to get an overview of it by reading it in its entirety. It is not long—only 61 verses. Your goal is to see how it is put together, to notice its atmosphere. This is not the time to answer every question that you might have. As you read, jot down in your notebook any questions that come to mind. They will probably be answered as we work our way through the text.

This is your assignment: Read 2 Peter through in one sitting. Always begin your time with prayer, asking God to reveal truth through His Holy Spirit. Then read, but not too fast. Read as if it is a letter from the apostle Peter to you personally. Enjoy your time with the Lord.

DAY TWO

In Bible study, we always start with the obvious. People, places, and events are always obvious. They are the easiest things to see. While they are not always the most important details of a book, they will lead us to the truth the author is trying to communicate. Today we will learn everything we can in chapter 1 about the author of 2 Peter.

Your assignment is to read chapter 1 slowly. As you read, mark every place the author refers to himself. In your notebook, list what you learn about the author when he mentions himself. You do this by asking the "who, what, when, where, why, and how" questions such as these:

Who is the author? (Peter 1:1) *Peter*

How does he describe himself? (a bond-servant and apostle of Jesus Christ, 1:1)

As you do this assignment, pay close attention to the pronoun *we* in verses 16-21.

DAY THREE

Today's assignment will be very much like yesterday's. Read chapters 2 and 3. As you read, note every place the author refers to himself and list in your notebook what you learn. Remember, it is by asking yourself the "who, what, when, where, why, and how" questions that you glean the information. Always start with prayer, asking God to show you truth as you read His Word.

By the way, Peter doesn't refer to himself at all in chapter 2, but we want you to read it anyway. The goal of these assignments is for you to become familiar with the book as

✱ writing to the Believers

a whole, not simply to gain information about Peter. Hang in there, friend, God has so much He wants to show you.

DAY FOUR

Are you in love with this letter yet? Second Peter is so incredibly relevant to Christianity today.

Today we will shift from the author to the recipients. Read chapter 1 and mark every reference to the recipients of this letter. We suggest shading each reference orange with a colored pencil. You will want to mark the plural pronouns *our* and *us*. Do not mark *we* in verses 12-21. Here Peter is referring to himself and the other apostles. We will study this passage in depth later.

When you have finished marking, list in your notebook what you learn about the recipients from chapter 1.

DAY FIVE

Read chapters 2 and 3. As you read, mark every reference to the recipients of this letter, just as you did in chapter 1 yesterday. List in your notebook everything you learn about them.

Remember, start with prayer and read slowly. You are dealing with the Word of God; your time shouldn't be rushed.

DAY SIX

You have put in a lot of work, but hasn't it been worth it? Remain diligent. You are mining pure gold.

Have you noticed Peter's purpose in writing? Knowing the author's purpose makes interpretation much easier. Today we want you to focus on two specific passages in 2 Peter that will help you see his purpose in writing. Read 1:12-21 and 3:1-3. As you read, mark every reference to *remind, remember* and its synonyms. When you have finished, record Peter's purpose for writing in your notebook.

Sometimes antonyms (words that mean the opposite of the original word) the author uses can give us insight into his meaning and purpose. After you have completed the above assignment, read 1:5-9. Watch for the antonym for "remembering." Record in your notebook any insight the text gives you.

Let me ask you, what does Peter want his readers to remember?

DAY SEVEN

 Store in your heart: 2 Peter 3:1-2.
Read and discuss: 2 Peter.

QUESTIONS FOR DISCUSSION OR INDIVIDUAL STUDY

- ❧ What is Peter's purpose in writing this letter? Of what does he want to remind them? Why?

- ❧ Do we need this reminder today? Why?

- ❧ According to chapter 3 what should we, as believers, remember? Why?

- ❧ How can you make this a part of your daily life? In other words, what action can you take to ensure you are following Peter's exhortation?

- When in Peter's life is he writing? How do you know?

- What else did you learn about Peter this week?

- To whom is Peter writing? How are they described?

- Take some time to compare your relationship with the Lord to the one Peter describes.

- Is the description of the recipients of this letter a description of the normal everyday Christian? If so, how are you doing?

- What did you learn about yourself this week?

THOUGHT FOR THE WEEK

Peter wants his readers to remember two things. First, he wants them to "remember the words spoken beforehand by the holy prophets." Second, he wants them to "remember the commandment of the Lord...spoken by your apostles." These two phrases remind me of the Old and New Testaments. He wants them to remember the Word of God. I am sure you have already seen the problem Peter is addressing in chapter 2. We will learn more about the false teachers in the next few weeks, but for now you have already seen the danger Peter is concerned about. The danger is just as real today.

What is your security? In a world full of conflicting claims, how will you know truth from error? With so many people claiming to speak for God, how do you know who is right? Friend, you need to become intimately acquainted with the "words spoken beforehand by the holy prophets" and the "commandment of the Lord." You need to connect to the one thing that is strong enough to keep you from falling. The safety line that will hold you in place is the

Word of God—both the Old and New Testaments. The Word is strong enough to hold you in place. You can trust it with your very life. It is eternal, life changing, and absolutely true. Stay connected to the truth.

We know this can seem like a daunting task. This is why we produce the New Inductive Study Series, and it is why we recommend *The New Inductive Study Bible*. These are great tools to keep you in the Word, learning at your own pace. You are doing great. Keep it up.

WALKING IN THE TRUTH

Have you ever been put off by someone who did not live what they said they believed? Does your personal walk match your talk? We all struggle with living up to what we know we should be, but the more we walk like Christ, the less offense we give to others around us. Is your walk helping others connect to the truth, or are you a hindrance? Think about the "roof" illustration we started with. Do the people around you trust you to help them connect to the truth, or would they rather just slide off the roof? Peter has a lot to say to us this week.

DAY ONE

Now that you have a good overview of 2 Peter, we will focus our study on chapter 1. You are probably glad the reading assignments will be shorter. Today your assignment is to read chapter 1 and mark every reference to the words *knowledge, know,* and *known.*[1] When you have finished marking, list in your notebook what you learn about knowledge from 2 Peter 1. As you read, pay close attention to the word *true* when it is used with *knowledge*. Ask yourself why Peter uses this phrase. What does he want us to know, and why?

Remember, start with prayer, asking God to reveal truth to you, and read slowly.

DAY TWO

Who is Jesus? Is He God? Does the Bible ever claim He is God, or does it really just say He had a special relationship with God?

It is a question that many people in our world ask. It is a question you will know the answer to today. This is part of your safety line. Read chapter 1. As you read, mark every reference to *Jesus*, including any personal pronouns. Mark every reference with the same symbol and color, whether it is *Lord, Christ,* or *Savior* as long as it refers to Jesus. This assignment can be a little difficult, so don't read too hastily.

Let me give you two helpful hints before you start. First, do not assume certain titles always refer to only a certain member of the trinity. For example, *God* does not always refer to the Father, and *Lord* does not always refer to Jesus. Context will tell you to whom the title is referring. Second, when the pronoun *He* or *His* is used, it generally refers to the last proper noun. These two hints will help in this assignment.

This is going to be an exciting and possibly eye-opening time. Enjoy yourself.

DAY THREE

Did you enjoy yesterday? Wasn't it exciting to see Jesus declared both God and Savior in verse 1? As you are doing this study there will probably be opportunity to share with others what you are learning. Be ready!

In the light of what you learned yesterday, what is your responsibility? Since He has granted you these magnificent promises, how then should you live? We will begin to answer that question today. Start by reading 1:1-11. When you have finished reading, list in your notebook the qualities Peter says you should have in your life. Leave room to add more information about each quality later.

Finally, before you leave this study for today, read over this list of qualities. Ask God to teach you about these and to make them evident in your life.

DAY FOUR

In verse 5 of chapter 1, Peter uses the phrase "applying all diligence."[2] Another way of phrasing this idea is "with every ounce of energy you have." Alongside what God has provided we are to supply these qualities with every ounce of energy we have. The word "supply"[3] in verse 5 is taken from a Greek word that means to provide over and beyond what could have ever been expected. Are you getting the idea that these are important to God? Let me ask you, are you working that hard to exhibit these qualities in your life?

We are going to do some cross-references today to help us further understand these qualities. The purpose of cross-referencing is to see what other passages of Scripture have to say about a particular subject you are studying. If you are unsure about the meaning of some of these words, look them up in an English dictionary. I do this from time to time, and it can really help. As you gain insight, add your information to the list you started yesterday.

Faith: Romans 10:17; Hebrews 10:35–11:3

Moral excellence (goodness or virtue): Philippians 4:8; 2 Peter 2:1-3,12-14 (Compare "moral excellence" with the lifestyle of the false teachers.)

Knowledge: Proverbs 1:1-7; 2:1-6

Are these qualities evident in your life?

DAY FIVE

Today you will continue cross-referencing the qualities in 2 Peter 1:5-8. When you have finished, take this list to the Lord in prayer. Ask Him if these things are evident in your life.

Self-control (or temperance): Galatians 5:22-23
Perseverance: Romans 5:3-4; James 1:3-4
Godliness: 1 Timothy 4:7-8

DAY SIX

Today we will complete the cross-referencing exercise we started on Day Four. First, look up these references and add any new insight you gain to the list in your notebook. Then read over your list and 2 Peter 1:1-11 again. What is the relationship between these qualities?

Brotherly kindness[4]: 1 Peter 1:22-23
(The English transliteration of the Greek word is *phil-adelphia*, brotherly love. It is a characteristic of fellowship.)

Love: 1 Corinthians 13
(This is unconditional love. It might be helpful to mark the word *love* in this passage. We draw a heart over the

word and shade it yellow for God's love, red for man's love.)

When you have finished, take a few moments to discuss these eight character qualities with God. Ask Him to show you where you might be lacking and where you need more practice. Then commit to Him to do your part and supply these qualities in your life. After all, you do remember what He has done for you, don't you?

DAY SEVEN

Store in your heart: 2 Peter 1:5-8.
Read and discuss: 2 Peter 1.

QUESTIONS FOR DISCUSSION OR INDIVIDUAL STUDY

∞ What did you learn about Jesus Christ this week? Who is Jesus according to Peter?

∞ Was there a really difficult time in your life that became peaceful when you were reminded of who Jesus is and what He has done for you? What happened?

∞ In 1:5-7 we are told to "supply" certain things. What are these? How many are there?

∞ What effect does the presence or absence of these have in the Christian life?

∞ Why would knowledge be important?

∞ You are very familiar with chapter 1 now. What does Peter want us to know?

∾ What knowledge is important if one already has faith? Where do believers find knowledge?

∾ Is there a relationship between moral excellence and knowledge?

∾ Define self-control.

∾ Is there a relationship between moral excellence, knowledge, and self-control?

∾ What is perseverance? Are you persevering? What habits could you build into your life that would enable you to persevere?

∾ What is godliness?

∾ Do you love? Are the characteristics of 1 Corinthians 13 manifest in your life? How can you diligently add this to your life?

∾ Are any of these qualities lacking in your life? Which ones? How do you know?

∾ How can you integrate these qualities into your relationship with others?

THOUGHT FOR THE WEEK

You learned about sanctification in 1 Peter. It has been said that sanctification is a work of God that believers cooperate in. The saying fits with what you learned this week. Those qualities you spent most of the week thinking about are the essential Christian virtues. You see in the list the sanctification process of a believer. It is a work of God to build these qualities in a person. Yet you learned the command is for us as believers to diligently add these qualities to our life. It is a work of God that demands the cooperation of the believer. It is fascinating to me that the list starts with faith and ends with love. Sounds like the Christian walk, doesn't it? We start with faith, and through faith, we grow in these virtues. Love is the crown, the ultimate virtue.

I want to talk for a moment about some of these virtues. Self-control is the exact opposite of the excesses of the false teachers. It is similar to self-discipline. The mind is in charge, not the body. The mind, fixed on Christ (Colossians 3:1-2), controls the body and brings it under submission. Are you controlling yourself?

Perseverance can be described as viewing time from God's perspective. You continue in faith, waiting on Christ's return, not being anxious or worried. Why? You know God is in control and He will accomplish His purpose right on time. We will talk a little more about the return of Christ later; for now it is enough to remember that this is one reason we persevere: He is on His way back.

Brotherly kindness is similar to brotherly love and should be a characteristic of your fellowship with other Christians. The Greek word for love used in 2 Peter 1:7 is *agape*. It is an unconditional self-sacrificing action. When we love, we consider others more important than ourselves. When we grasp this, it revolutionizes the way we respond to everyone around us. Do you see others as more important than yourself? Are you sacrificing yourself for your family? For your friends?

When we work at making these virtues a vital part of who we are, we are offering a safety line to those around us. When we care about people, when we show them love, they are willing to listen to our message of hope. The old adage is true: People don't care how much you know until they know how much you care.

Work on these qualities in your life. Master these virtues. You will keep someone close to you from sliding off the roof because they are willing to listen to love and connect to the truth, the safety line.

THE GOD-GIVEN TRUTH

What is the basis for our belief? What are we tied to that will hold us in place? What must we know to be able to live with discernment in these end times? These are the questions we will answer this week as we look closely at 2 Peter.

DAY ONE

You learned last week about our growth in Christ as believers. Today we will see the grounds of our belief. What is the foundation of our faith? What is the basis for the "true knowledge" Peter has presented? In other words, how do I know the statements he has made are true and valid? Is there any evidence, or has he developed some cleverly devised tale?

Your assignment is to read carefully chapter 1:12-21 and watch for the evidence Peter presents. When you have finished, read Matthew 16:27–17:9. This will give you Matthew's version of what happened.

DAY TWO

Did you see the evidence Peter presents? First, he mentions his own eyewitness account, and second, the sure word of prophecy. Eyewitness accounts are extremely powerful in a court of law. I realize in this day of skepticism the question will arise, How do I know he was telling me the truth about being an eyewitness? Peter died, as did Paul, during Nero's persecution of Christians. Tradition tells us Peter was crucified upside down. Would a man *knowingly* die for a lie? Would you?

Peter is telling us that even more sure than his experience is the prophetic word, or Scripture. Today we will look a little closer at the prophetic word. Your assignment is to read 1:16-21 and mark two different but closely related terms. Mark the words *prophecy* and *prophetic* in a distinctive way, and mark each reference to *word* or *Scripture*. They are synonyms in this passage. Now, finish up your time by listing in your notebook what you learn about Scripture and prophecy in this passage. Finally, on your AT A GLANCE CHART for 2 Peter write down the theme for chapter 1.

We are simply not able to answer all of your questions concerning the reliability of Scripture in this format, but we will discuss it a little more tomorrow and the next day.

DAY THREE

The passage you observed yesterday is one of the classic passages that argue for divine inspiration of the Word of God. Today, I want you to read 2 Timothy 3:16-17. In your notebook, add to the list on Scripture you started yesterday. In a regular English dictionary look up the word *inspired* (*inspiration* in KJV). If you are studying from the New International Version, your text already gives the sense of the passage.

We want you to see how strong and secure your safety line is, my friend. You are doing an awesome job; hang in there. By the way, has anyone told you today God loves you?

DAY FOUR

Today we will wrap up our study on the authority of Scripture by looking at one incident in Luke that will show us Jesus' attitude toward the Word of God. He is the ultimate authority. Your assignment is to read, slowly and carefully, Luke 24:13-35. This story takes place immediately after the resurrection. When you have finished, answer in your notebook two questions.

1. Why did Jesus rebuke the two men?

2. What did He use to correct them?

DAY FIVE

I would love to continue to study the inspiration and the authority of the Word with you, but we must move on.

I know you have already noticed the false teachers mentioned in chapter 2. For the next two days, we will see exactly what Peter tells us about them. Today, your assignment is to read 2:1-10 and mark in a distinctive fashion every reference to the false teachers. When you have finished, start a list in your notebook of what you learn about the false teachers.

DAY SIX

Today's assignment is just like yesterday's, except you will start in verse 11 and work your way through verse 22.

When you are finished, you will have a complete description of the actions and characteristics of the false teachers. We will talk more about them next week.

DAY SEVEN

Store in your heart: 2 Peter 1:20-21.
Read and discuss: 2 Peter 1:12–2:22.

QUESTIONS FOR DISCUSSION OR INDIVIDUAL STUDY

∾ What has the Lord shown you this week?

∾ What does Peter give as the basis for our beliefs?

∾ How important does Peter consider our experience to be in validating truth? Are our experiences to be ignored? Are they to define our life? Why? Why not?

∾ What tool is available to validate our experience?

∾ What did you learn about the inspiration of the Word this week?

∾ How did Paul describe Scripture in 2 Timothy? What difference did this make in your life?

∾ What steps can you take to make Scripture a part of your daily life? Your family's life?

∾ What did you learn about Jesus' attitude toward Scripture? Did He believe it was accurate?

∾ Why did Jesus rebuke the men on the road to Emmaus? What had they not done? How does your understanding of and attitude toward the Scriptures differ from theirs?

THOUGHT FOR THE WEEK

In 1:19, Peter is essentially saying, "If you don't believe me, check out the Scriptures." The holy Word of God is more valid than any experience. We need to hear this today. We live in a society that runs on feelings, not necessarily on fact. Every week there is one more person telling the Christian community about a new experience he or she had, often claiming we must have it also. Well, Peter had an experience none of us could top. He saw the Lord in all of His light and glory! He saw the Lord transfigured! And if that was not enough, Peter also heard the audible voice of God speaking from heaven. Now that is an experience! Peter then states in 1:19 that Scripture is even more certain than his experience and that we should be careful to pay attention to the Word. Friend, more than anything else, we want you to pay close attention to the Word; it is a lamp shining in the darkness.

No prophecy is a matter of one's own interpretation because it does not originate with man; it originates with the Holy Spirit of God. The Greek word for Spirit is *pneuma*, which literally means a current of air. In a sense, the Holy Spirit is the breath of God. God spoke or breathed, and men moved by the Spirit wrote down the words of God. How trustworthy is the Bible? It is completely, totally, absolutely trustworthy!

If you have *The New Inductive Study Bible*, it contains a great article titled "Understanding the Value of God's Word" on page 2083 that will give you additional insight into the accuracy and trustworthiness of Scripture.

How strong is your safety line? If it's the Word of God, it's unbreakable. Trust the Word. It will hold you in place; it will keep you from sliding off into absolute nonsense. Stay connected to the Word of God.

SPOTTING FALSE TEACHERS

Peter calls them false teachers. They slip into the church and present another gospel. They claim to have a special knowledge. They have a new and improved safety line. Theirs will supposedly hold me better than ever. But will it? Friend, do not untie yourself from the Word of God; what they are offering will not hold. You will see what I mean this week.

DAY ONE

Last week we began to look at the false teachers. This week we will study chapter 2 more closely. We want you to see the flow of thought from chapter 1 to chapter 2. Remember, Peter did not write in chapter and verse; he wrote a letter.

Today, I want you to read 2 Peter 1:12–2:22. As you read, pay close attention to the word "but" in verse 1—it indicates a contrast. Contrasts are often used by the Holy Spirit to teach us a truth. Watch for what is being contrasted between the last few verses of chapter 1 and the beginning verses of chapter 2. Mark the words *destructive* and *destruction*[5] in chapter 2. I use a red squiggly line through the word.

You are starting with prayer, aren't you? Read slowly—Peter is warning you personally.

DAY TWO

What is the danger you face from these false teachers? What is the danger they face? Today, read chapter 2 again, and this time list in your notebook everything you learned by marking *destructive* and *destruction*. You probably understood this information when you were learning about the false teachers in week three, but looking at the material from a different perspective can sometimes give new insights.

DAY THREE

You have seen that God will judge the false teachers. The fact that God doesn't always judge immediately does not mean that He approves; it means that—oh, we'll study that next week.

Today, let's study the lifestyle of false teachers by cross-referencing to 2 Corinthians 11. As a matter of background information, Paul is defending his ministry against false teachers in chapters 10–13 of this letter. Read 2 Corinthians 11:1-4,12-15, and add to your list what you learn about false teachers. When you are finished, think about this question: Where are the false teachers? Outside the church, or inside? Or both?

DAY FOUR

We have seen the danger posed by the false teachers in 2:1-3 and their promised destruction in 2:4-10. But what do they look like? Are there characteristics that would help me identify them? Yes there are—they are characterized by greed and sensuality.

Read the following passages and note what you learn about greed and sensuality.

- ∾ Colossians 3:5

- ∾ Romans 13:13-14

- ∾ Galatians 5:19-21, 22-24 (Watch for the contrast.)

DAY FIVE

I realize yesterday's assignment was a little long, but it is very important that you see the truth for yourself. There are teachers within churches today whose lifestyles don't match up with the pursuit of godliness. You need to see what the false teachers look like in order to avoid their traps. Read 2 Peter 2 again. This time, ask yourself how the false teachers will try to lead you astray. What are you being warned about? How will they entice you? What will they do?

DAY SIX

Today we will move on to chapter 3. Your assignment is to read chapter 3 and mark every reference to *destroyed* and *destruction*[6] just as you did in chapter 2. In your notebook, list what you learn from chapter 3.

Just reading chapter 3 can raise a lot of questions about things like "day of God." Don't become sidetracked. We will work our way through this next week.

DAY SEVEN

 Store in your heart: 2 Peter 2:1.
Read and discuss: 2 Peter 2.

QUESTIONS FOR DISCUSSION OR INDIVIDUAL STUDY

∾ What did you learn about destruction this week as you studied chapter 2?

∾ Where would you find false teachers today?

∾ What does a false teacher look like? How would you recognize one?

∾ Compare "moral excellence" with the lifestyle of the false prophets described in 2 Peter. What do you see?

∾ Evaluate popular teachings put forth in the name of God today. What or where is the emphasis? Is the emphasis ever on money or prosperity?

∾ Do you see any common denominators between some of today's "Christian" messages and the messages of false prophets of 2 Peter?

∾ When someone uses the Bible to prove their point, are you familiar enough with the Word of God to know whether or not that person is handling Scripture properly? He may be speaking the truth, but does the passage he is handling mean what he says it means? Can you tell? Why or why not?

∾ How important to God is your lifestyle? As long as you believe, it doesn't matter how you live—or does it?

THOUGHT FOR THE WEEK

In reference to 2 Peter 2:20-22 the questions sometimes arise, Are these false teachers believers who have lost their salvation? Are they believers who are deceived? These are good questions, valid ones, that we will try to answer today and in next week's study.

Take a moment to look back over your list of the characteristics of the false prophets. What are they doing according to 2 Peter 2:1? Who are they denying? The word "denying" is in the present tense in the Greek. (As you know, the New Testament was originally written in Greek. Sometimes it can be very helpful to look at the Greek words and the grammatical structure behind the English translation to get a clearer idea of what the author is trying to communicate.) The present tense indicates that this was an ongoing pattern of their life and teaching, not a one-time event. I ask again, Who are they constantly denying? The Greek word for "bought" is in the aorist tense, which simply means "at some point in time." The price of their redemption had been paid, but they had not accepted it. They were constantly denying the master.

These teachers had a knowledge of God and even fled from or escaped the defilements of the world. The phrase "escaped the defilements" indicates they cleaned up their act. It doesn't necessarily mean they were born again. In verse 22 Peter uses the terms "dog" and "sow" to describe their state. Both of these animals were unclean to the Jewish people. Did you notice neither animal was changed? Both came back to doing what they would normally do.

The picture of the Christian life is one of being born again—old things have passed away; all things have become new. They were never born again, they were just washed on the outside.

Peter uses the term "false words" to describe the message of the false teachers. The Greek word translated "false" is *plastos*. It is the root of our English word "plastic." It means molded or shaped. The idea is that they mold or shape their words to fit the occasion. They sound smooth and reasonable. The danger is great. If I don't know what the words mean, how can I know the truth?

This really hit home with me when I was discussing the resurrection of Christ with someone. We both used the term, but I did not find out until later we defined it differently. I was discussing a Jesus who is physically raised from the dead. He was talking about a Jesus who was only symbolically raised in your heart when you believe. He was using plastic words that could be molded to fit any situation. Friend, please be careful. Satan hates you and has a horrible plan for your life. Know the truth; know the Word of God. We encourage you to stay in Bible study—don't stop!

How safe am I if my safety line is made of soft, moldable, pliable plastic? Be careful what you connect yourself to.

BEWARE OF THOSE WHO MOCK GOD'S PROMISE AND HIS JUDGMENT

Do not be deceived. God will not be mocked. When He says He will do something, He will. He is the promise-keeping God. If He said He is coming back, He is. Are you ready?

DAY ONE

This is our last week together in 2 Peter. Can you believe it? Our prayer is that God will so reveal Himself to you during this study of 1 Peter, 2 Peter, and Jude that you will never be the same again. We want you to be in love with His Word.

Today read 2 Peter 3 and mark every reference to *know* and *knowing*[7] just as you did in chapter 1. When you have finished, add to your notebook what you learn. Peter uses these words to give two commands. If you read carefully, these words will show you the essence of the chapter. Slow down; follow the flow of thought. Did you see the two commands that establish the parameters of the chapter? Peter is warning the readers about the mockers.

DAY TWO

Who are the mockers? What are they saying? How do I respond?

We will try to answer these questions today from 2 Peter. Read chapter 3, and as you do, mark every reference to the mockers and review your markings of *destroyed* and *destruction* (Week 4, Day 6, page 83). Then list what you learn about the mockers.

Notice what was destroyed and how and when it happened. Then look at what will be destroyed, when it will happen, and how. I know you have read this chapter several times already, but each time you go over the text, you open yourself up to the Word and to the possibility of the Holy Spirit showing you something new. The Word is rich. Read it one more time. Read it after you pray, asking the Holy Spirit to lead you into truth.

DAY THREE

"Promises, promises." You have heard the phrase, haven't you? The mockers were saying the same thing. They were basically atheistic in their approach to life. "It doesn't matter what we do; God will not do anything about it. He's not going to judge us! Never has, never will." But is that true?

Today, read 2 Peter 3 and mark the word *promise*. When you have finished, list everything you learn about promises in this chapter.

DAY FOUR

"The day of the Lord," "the day of judgment," and "the day of God" all refer to the same period of time. We cannot answer all of your questions about the day of the Lord in this study, but 2 Peter 3 does give us some answers. Read 2 Peter 3 and underline *His coming* (NIV: *this 'coming'*) and *the day of.*[8] Then list in your notebook what you learn from this passage about the day of the Lord. Pay close attention to the purpose of the day of the Lord.

DAY FIVE

You probably still have a lot of questions about the day of the Lord. Again, we can't answer them all in this study. But you have seen the basics.

We are wrapping up our time in 2 Peter. You have worked hard and dug out truth for yourself, and we are so proud of you. You have persevered to this point, and we trust you will continue on. It pleases God to have you in His Word, getting to know Him. Keep your focus on Him.

Now that we have looked at this letter paragraph by paragraph, line by line, we need to look at the whole letter one more time to be sure we see the flow of thought. Your assignment today is to read 2 Peter. Don't mark anything or make any lists. Just read and watch the flow of thought. Ignore (if that is possible) the verse numbers and the chapter breaks. Just read it as if it were a letter from Peter to you. Enjoy your time.

DAY SIX

You are finished with 2 Peter. I realize we did not answer all of your questions. But you do have a handle on the overview of this little letter. You have seen the flow of thought. You learned about the basic Christian virtues. You have learned about false teachers, their attitudes and actions. You have learned about the mockers and the day of the Lord. You have handled a lot of information. Today I want you to read the last two verses of this letter. Note what God calls you and what you are to do. Are you doing it?

Spend your time in prayer. Ask God to show you what He wants you to leave this study with. Ask Him what changes need to be made in your life. Ask Him if any of the attitudes of the false teachers or the mockers are true in your life. Ask Him to show you how you can continue to grow in His grace and in the knowledge of Him. Thank Him for His love and His Word. Enjoy your time with Him.

Now live in the light of the promise of Jesus' coming. Be about God's business. Jesus hasn't come yet because there are more to be saved. Maybe you would introduce that final one to Jesus Christ!

DAY SEVEN

 Store in your heart: 2 Peter 3:17-18.
Read and discuss: 2 Peter 3.

QUESTIONS FOR DISCUSSION OR INDIVIDUAL STUDY

- Specifically from your study of chapter 3, what does Peter want you to know? What are the warnings he gives?

- Describe the mockers. Are there mockers today? What are they denying?

- How should we respond to them?

- Do men today deny the flood as a historical fact? Men outside the church? Inside? Do you deny the flood? If you deny it, what are you denying?

૭ Do you believe the promise of His coming?

૭ What did you learn about God's patience? What did you learn about His heart? What is God's heart's desire?

૭ What did you learn about the day of the Lord? What is the purpose of the day of the Lord?

૭ In light of what you have learned about the day of the Lord, what is your responsibility?

THOUGHT FOR THE WEEK

Are you waiting with expectancy for the coming day of the Lord? Do you really expect Him back, or in reality are you more like the mockers who did not believe His promise that He would return? Practically speaking, do you live like you believe in the day of the Lord?

Dr. Wayne Barber, former pastor of Woodland Park Baptist Church in Chattanooga, Tennessee, tells the story of being asked to preach at a school assembly. When he arrived with all of his outlines and sermon notes, he discovered that the school was a special boarding school for mentally handicapped children. He realized his notes were of no value; the students would never comprehend the complicated outlines. He prayed and asked God for wisdom. Feeling led of the Lord, he began to read verses of Scripture to them. As he read, the children began to shout "Jesus, Jesus" over and over. They had an intense love for the Lord.

When his time was over, Wayne commented to the principal about how much the children loved Jesus. The principal's reply was, "Yes. We can't keep the windows clean on the east side of the building." Wayne did not understand, so the principal explained. It seems someone had told the children Jesus was coming back someday and that He would come from the east. Every morning the children go to the east side of the building and press their hands and faces against the windows, looking to see if Jesus is coming.

Are you waiting for His return with the same faith and expectancy those children have?

He is coming. How then should you act? Grow in the grace and knowledge of our Lord and Savior Jesus Christ.

2 PETER AT A GLANCE

Theme of 2 Peter:

	Paragraph Themes	Chapter Themes	Author:
	1:1-11	1	
	1:12-15		Historical Setting:
	1:16-18		Purpose:
	1:19-21		
	2:1-3	2	Key Words:
	2:4-10		
	2:11-16		
	2:17-22		
	3:1-7	3	
	3:8-10		
	3:11-13		
	3:14-18		

JUDE

WARNINGS ABOUT FALSE TEACHERS

Have you ever stopped to take a good look at all those who profess to believe in Jesus Christ, those who hang around the church or church folks and say they are sure they are going to heaven? Do you see a disparity—a dichotomy—a contradiction between the way they live and the way other seemingly dedicated Christians live?

Are they genuine believers, or could they be deceived? If they are deceived or flat-out lying, are they any danger to the church? And what should be your response or responsibility with respect to them and what they proclaim with their lips and their lives?

You are about to discover encouraging, enlightening, yet sobering answers to these questions in the 25 verses that comprise the little book of Jude. And as you do, you will find yourself amazed at the spiritual gems in this book. You'll be richer spiritually and intellectually for having studied it.

CONTENDING FOR THE TRUTH

How well do you know the Word of God, and how quick are *you* to defend its precepts? Or is the question irrelevant for those who sit in the pew rather than stand in the pulpit? It's a good question to answer now, before you meet God face-to-face.

DAY ONE

Every book of the Bible has its own unique purpose. Understanding the reason a book was written helps us understand why it is included in God's holy Bible. Jude is no exception. Its message is extremely relevant and urgently needed in our times.

Read through Jude, and as you do, mark every reference to the author of this short epistle. If you don't know how to do this, or can't really decide, we recommend that you use the suggested markings from *The New Inductive Study Bible* (*NISB*). The *NISB* suggests that whenever marking a book, you always color the references to the author, including all nouns and pronouns, in blue. Whatever—mark the references so you can easily spot the author's name and any pronouns that refer to him (in this case, "I").

When you finish, put a heading in your notebook, INSIGHTS ON THE AUTHOR OF JUDE. Then list what you learn about the author from having marked the text.

When you finish your list, you will see the author's purpose in writing. Record the author's purpose on the JUDE AT A GLANCE chart on page 112 in the designated place.

DAY TWO

Read through Jude again today. Read it as if it were written to you. In the sovereignty of God, it was! It is important for people to have this message in every generation. God included it in the Bible so you could order your life accordingly.

As you read, mark every reference to the recipients (including all the synonyms and personal pronouns). If you don't have a color in mind, try orange as recommended in the *NISB*.

When you finish, list everything you learn about the recipients. You need not record any instructions at this point, only those things that would give you insight into who they are and what their future is.

DAY THREE

It's an interesting little book, isn't it?! Did you notice that there is another group of people referred to in this letter? It's the "certain persons" first mentioned in verse 4. Read through Jude a third time—reading it aloud will help you remember what Jude is all about. This time, mark every reference to *these men,* these *certain persons.*[1] Try brown if you don't know what color to use.

DAY FOUR

Yesterday, you marked the references to the "certain persons" who crept in unnoticed; today, list everything you learn about them from the text.

Observe where these people are, and then think about the church in general—those who profess to be Christians. Are these kind of people around today? Think about it.

DAY FIVE

Read Jude, verses 1-8 aloud, and underline the word *remind*.[2] When you finish, list in your notebook what Jude wants to remind them about.

Did you notice the words *destroyed*,[3] *judgment*,[4] and *eternal fire*? Mark these in a distinctive way. Maybe color them red with a mark like this ///////.

Now circle *angels* and any pronouns that refer to them, and then connect the circles with a line.

What do you learn from marking the references to the angels? List it in your notebook under ANGELS.

DAY SIX

Review Jude 5-8 again aloud. What does the text tell you about Sodom and Gomorrah and the cities around them? List everything you learn about them in your notebook under the heading, SODOM AND GOMORRAH.

Now read Genesis 19:1-29. In Genesis 18 God warns Abraham that the outcry of Sodom and Gomorrah's sin is great and that He is going to investigate their sin. What did the two angels sent by God discover? What happened to Sodom and Gomorrah and why? Record it in your notebook and then compare it with what you observed in Jude.

What do you learn from simply observing the text of the Bible in Genesis 19 and Jude 7? Do you see any application to today?

Now, whom is God going to bring judgment upon in

Jude 5 and why?

Jude 6 and why?

Jude 7 and why?

Write it in your notebook.

DAY SEVEN

 Store in your heart: Jude 3.
Read and discuss: Jude 1-7.

QUESTIONS FOR DISCUSSION OR INDIVIDUAL STUDY

∞ What did you learn about Jude as a person?

∞ What was his reason for writing this short epistle? Was this what he intended to write when he began? What had he intended to write? What did he write? Discuss the general content of Jude.

∞ What did you learn from marking the references to the recipients of this letter? Does what you learn about them have any application to genuine believers today? Discuss this.

∞ What did you learn from marking the references to the *certain persons* in verse 4? Make sure you note where these persons can be found. What application does this have to our times?

~ Jude reminds the recipients of his letter of three things in verses 5, 6, and 7. What are they? Discuss them verse by verse.

~ What do these three groups have in common in respect to their future?

~ What do you learn from this week's study about homosexuality? What does the Word of God say?

~ How do the "certain persons" in verse 4 compare with the personages mentioned in verses 5-7—what commonality is there between them?

~ Discuss any instructions that are given to the recipients of this letter in verses 1-8 and any application it has to us today. Is this for those in the pulpit or those in the pew?

~ Discuss the most significant insight the various members of the group gained in their study this week.

THOUGHT FOR THE WEEK

In a time when political correctness is in vogue, an individual can seem very narrow-minded and obtrusive when he or she is not generously inclusive or syncretistic about religious matters. There is one Scripture the world seems to have learned and loves to quote even in the words of the old King James translation: "Judge not, that ye be not judged."

The world does not want us to have any opinions regarding who is going to go to heaven and who is going to the punishment of eternal fire. Who are we to judge? Many people who pull this verse (Matthew 7:1) out of context and twist it to their own destruction don't understand that not everyone who says, "Lord, Lord" is a genuine believer. Only those who hear His words and do them will enter the kingdom of heaven (Matthew 7:21).

Jude makes it very clear that the *visible* church is not only comprised of those who are the called, the beloved of God, the kept for Jesus Christ, but also with those who have "crept in unnoticed." They are the ungodly living among the godly who say we can live any way we want (licentiously) and still go to heaven. God forbid! And that is exactly what He does in this epistle. God sets us straight with the truth.

These are persons who will never go to heaven. A righteous God who destroyed those who came out of Egypt but did not really believe God, and who has kept angels in eternal bonds because they did not keep their own domain in the days of Noah and indulged in gross immorality (just like the men of Sodom and Gomorrah did) will also consign these ungodly persons to eternal condemnation.

And what is our responsibility, whether in the pulpit or in the pew? It is to be "biblically correct" rather than politically correct. We are instructed to earnestly contend ("contend" is in the present tense) as a habit of life for the faith, the Word of God delivered to us in its entirety. Those who profess to be believers must understand that no one can live licentiously (without absolutes, without parameters) and go to heaven. Those who believe otherwise do not know the Word of God, the holiness of the God of the Word, nor the power of salvation that frees every true believer from slavery to sin. The life of a genuine Christian is in juxtaposition to those who merely confess Him with their lips but deny Him with their lives.

The question is, where do you stand? Does your life evidence a genuine salvation? And if so, Beloved, how valiant are you in standing for truth? If not, why not? It's an important question to answer now while you can line up your life with the plumb line of God's Word and be prepared to see God face-to-face.

DISTINGUISHING THE UNGODLY FROM THE GODLY

How does one distinguish the godly from the ungodly? And what is the responsibility of the godly to those who have not believed? These are questions that will be answered in this final week as you observe the inerrant Word of God—words of life that when obeyed bring abundant life.

DAY ONE

Since you have the luxury of studying a short epistle, read through Jude aloud not only to refresh your memory as to the content of this book, but also to help etch it in your memory.

Now review the list of observations you recorded about ungodly persons from verse 8.

According to verse 8, what three things do these men do in the same manner as the personages mentioned in verses 5-7? Number them in your Bible, or list them in your notebook.

Then note how—according to verse 8—they do it. Are they dealing with reality? Dreaming is a present participle, which implies continuous or habitual action.

How does the action of these men in verse 8 relate to verses 9 and 10? Mark the word *revile*.[5] Also note the contrast in verse 10 between what they revile and what they know by instinct.

How do you live? What governs what you do? Is your life governed by truth, the Word of God, or by instinct, dreaming, and delusion? What do you need to do to make sure that it's governed by truth?

DAY TWO

In verse 4, we saw that certain persons "turn the grace of our God into licentiousness"[6] (saying that because you are saved by grace, you can live any way you want and still go to heaven) and "deny our only Master and Lord, Jesus Christ." In verse 11, we see that they have gone the way of Cain. What does that mean?

Read Genesis 4 and mark every reference to Cain. Then list what you learn about Cain. Note the life consequences of Cain's refusal to offer the kind of sacrifice God wanted. What does this tell you? Think about it, and record your insights in your notebook.

Now read Hebrews 11:4, and note what you learn about Cain's sacrifice versus Abel's. If Abel offered his sacrifice in faith, then it was a sacrifice that was in accordance with God's Word. Jude says the ungodly went the way of Cain. From all you have observed, record what you think that way would be. What would that look like in the visible church today?

DAY THREE

God tells us through Jude that the ungodly men that have crept in unnoticed among the believers have rushed headlong into the error of Balaam and perished in the rebellion of Korah (verse 11).

Balaam was a prophet for hire who wanted to curse the children of God but found he could not curse a people whom God had blessed. Therefore, he suggested that, if Balaak wanted God to move against His people, they should get the daughters of Moab to seduce the men of Israel and thereby incur the judgment of God. The whole account is recorded in Numbers 22–25:9 and 31:1-20. If you have the time to read it, you will find it not only interesting but enlightening and pertinent to our lives.

The rebellion of Korah is recorded in Numbers 16. Read this chapter, examining it in the light of the 5 W's and an H: who, what, when, where, why, and how. See what you can learn about Korah's rebellion. List your insights in your notebook.

DAY FOUR

Read through Jude 10-19 today and take a fresh look at the ungodly men who crept in among the believers unnoticed. (If you have already studied 2 Peter, you will see many parallels in these verses with the false teachers and mockers who are described in that short epistle.) Observe how they are described in verses 12-13. Note the metaphors and the point God is making through Jude. Mark every reference to eternal destruction just like you did in the first eight verses of Jude.

In verses 14-16, you get an interesting insight about Enoch that isn't recorded any other place in the Bible.

Note the description of the men in verses 16, 18, and 19. Think about the message their behavior gives and the problems it can cause; then examine yourself and see if any of these actions and attitudes have crept into your life. Spend time in prayer asking God to search your heart and cleanse your life with the water of His Word.

DAY FIVE

Now comes a pleasant switch! Read Jude 17-25 and list again what you observe about the beloved. This time, watch for any instructions. You might want to write "Instruction" in the margin of your Bible next to any verse in which you find an instruction. As you observe verses 20 and 21, look at the specific instructions that tell them how to keep themselves in the love of God. Are there any of these instructions you need to put into action?

Keep (kept) is a key word in this epistle. Read through Jude again and mark its every occurrence. The original word (except in verse 24) is *tereo* and means to watch over. What do you learn from marking "kept" and "keep"?

Finally, note the contrast in these verses between the beloved and the ungodly living among them.

DAY SIX

Read Jude 22-23 thoughtfully. List the three different classes or conditions of people, and list the instructions to the believers regarding each one. Then record what your responsibility is in respect to each one.

What do you learn about God and about Jesus in the last two verses of Jude?

The Greek word translated "keep" in verse 24 is *phulasso* and means to guard.

Compare Jude 24 with Ephesians 1:4; 5:27; Philippians 1:10; 2:15; Colossians 1:22; and 1 Thessalonians 5:23. Read them in context and then note what you learn about being holy and blameless from these verses. Do you see any relationship between Jude 20-21 and verse 24? Does the Christian have anything to do with being blameless, or is a holy and blameless condition simply bestowed upon every believer?

Consider your life in the light of these truths to see how well your life conforms to His precepts.

Finally, fill in your JUDE AT A GLANCE chart on page 112 and you will have a nice summary of the content of Jude.

DAY SEVEN

Store in your heart: Jude 20-21 or 24-25.
Read and discuss: Jude 9-25.

QUESTIONS FOR DISCUSSION OR INDIVIDUAL STUDY

∾ What do you learn about the ungodly from verses 8-10? How would this help you discern what the ungodly are like so you are not influenced by them?

∾ What does it mean to:
   • go the way of Cain?
   • rush headlong into the error of Balaam?
   • perish in the rebellion of Korah?

∾ What danger do the ungodly pose to the church?

∾ What is the future of the ungodly men mentioned in Jude? How does this compare with the future of the godly (the beloved)?

∾ What do you learn about the judgment of God from this epistle? Summarize it by looking at all the references to it in Jude.

∾ What are the instructions given to the beloved in this epistle?

∾ Is there anything relevant in these instructions for today? How can they be practically applied? Discuss this.

∾ Are there any instructions given to the church as to how they are to deal with the ungodly that have crept in among them?

∾ What is the most significant thing you learned from Jude? Did God convict you in respect to anything? Did He comfort or encourage you in any way?

THOUGHT FOR THE WEEK

We may not be able to purge the church of the ungodly who creep in unnoticed, but we certainly can recognize them by their behavior and protect others from them. That protection comes when we uphold the veracity of God's Word and stand firm against error. Or to put it in Jude's words, "contend earnestly for the faith."

To do that we must continually build ourselves up on our most holy faith by studying the Word of God, even as you are doing through this study. We must also keep ourselves in the love of God by loving Him and obeying His commandments. Jesus said if we love Him we will obey Him. And of course, prayer is crucial. We must stay in communication with God, praying in the Holy Spirit: seeking His help and His wisdom, laboring in prayer on behalf of all the saints and the furtherance of His kingdom.

Our Lord's return and the certainty that we will be like Him when we see Him should ever be on our heart and mind so that rather than being entangled with the affairs of this life, we are anxiously awaiting His coming.

And of course, because we live for God and are ambassadors of Christ who have been given the ministry of reconciliation, getting the gospel to the lost should always be foremost on our heart. Without Him, people will perish.

We must be merciful with those who doubt, helping them in their weakness. And we must faithfully warn those who we know are headed for eternal damnation seeking to snatch them from the fire. They must know that without Jesus Christ and the righteousness He gives, they will surely perish.

And those who reek with the pollution of the world are not to be scorned or despised but treated with mercy. Yes, we must be careful that we despise their sin so that in rescuing them we are not tempted; nevertheless they need mercy and rescuing, and this we must do, Beloved, in the fear of the Lord. There is no other to whom belongs eternal glory, majesty, dominion, and authority!

May we live accordingly so that when we see Him, we will be blameless and filled with joy.

Theme of Jude:

SEGMENT
DIVISIONS

Author:

		PARAGRAPH THEMES
		VERSES 1, 2
		VERSES 3, 4
		VERSES 5-7
		VERSES 8-13
		VERSES 14-16
		VERSES 17-23
		VERSES 24, 25

Historical Setting:

Purpose:

Key Words:

Notes

1 PETER

1. KJV, NKJV: *begotten;* NIV: *given…new birth*
2. ESV, NKJV: *grieved;* KJV: *in heaviness;* NIV: *suffer grief*
3. KJV: *tried;* NIV: *refined*
4. NIV: *spiritual*
5. NKJV: *grow up thereby*
6. KJV: *Wherefore;* ESV: *So*
7. KJV: *guile*
8. KJV, NKJV: *evil speaking(s)*
9. KJV: *believeth;* NIV: *trusts*
10. NIV: *message*
11. KJV, NKJV: *good works*
12. ESV, NKJV: *do good;* KJV: *do well*
13. ESV, NIV, NKJV: *doing good;* KJV: *well doing*
14. KJV: sometimes *afflictions*
15. ESV, KJV: *subject;* NIV: *submit*
16. KJV, NKJV, ESV: *likewise*
17. NIV: *in the (his) body; earthly life, in regard to the body*
18. KJV, NKJV, NIV, ESV: *God*

2 PETER

1. NIV: *told you; understand*
2. ESV, NIV: *make every effort;* KJV, NKJV: *giving all diligence*
3. ESV: *supplement;* KJV, NIV, NKJV: *add*
4. ESV: *brotherly affection*
5. KJV: *damnation, overthrow;* NIV: *perish;* ESV: *extinction*
6. KJV: *damnation, overthrow;* NIV: *perish;* ESV: *extinction*
7. ESV: *understand*
8. KJV, NIV, NKJV: *forever*

JUDE

1. KJV, NKJV, NIV: *certain men;* ESV: *certain people; these people;* KJV: *these filthy dreamers;* NKJV, NIV: *these dreamers*
2. KJV: *put in remembrance*
3. KJV, NKJV: sometimes *corrupt*
4. KJV, NIV, NKJV: sometimes *accusation*
5. ESV: *blaspheme;* KJV, NKJV: *speak evil;* NIV: *slander*
6. ESV: *sensuality;* KJV: *lasciviousness;* NIV: *license for immorality;* NKJV: *lewdness*

NOTES FOR PERSONAL STUDY

NOTES FOR PERSONAL STUDY

NOTES FOR PERSONAL STUDY

NOTES FOR PERSONAL STUDY

NOTES FOR PERSONAL STUDY

NOTES FOR PERSONAL STUDY

NOTES FOR PERSONAL STUDY

NOTES FOR PERSONAL STUDY

NOTES FOR PERSONAL STUDY

NOTES FOR PERSONAL STUDY

NOTES FOR PERSONAL STUDY

Books in the
New Inductive Study Series

❧❧❧❧

Do you want a life that thrives?

Wherever you are on your spiritual journey, there is a way to discover Truth for yourself so you can find the abundant life in Christ.

Kay Arthur, David Lawson, and Bob Vereen invite you to join them on the ultimate journey. Learn to live life God's way by knowing Him through His Word.

❧

Visit www.precept.org/thrives
to take the next step by
downloading a free study tool.

PRECEPT
MINISTRIES
INTERNATIONAL
THE ❦ INDUCTIVE BIBLE STUDY PEOPLE

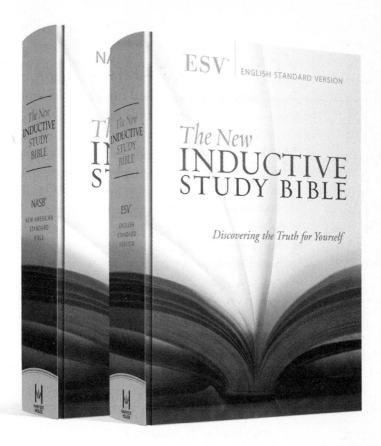

DIGGING DEEPER

Books in the New Inductive Study Series are survey courses. If you want to do a more in-depth study of a particular book of the Bible, we suggest that you do a Precept Upon Precept Bible Study Course on that book. The Precept studies require approximately five hours of personal study a week. You may obtain more information on these powerful courses by contacting Precept Ministries International at 800-763-8280, visiting our website at www.precept.org, or filling out and mailing the response card in the back of this book.

If you desire to expand and sharpen your skills, you would really benefit by attending a Precept Ministries Institute of Training. The Institutes are conducted throughout the United States, Canada, and in a number of other countries. Class lengths vary from one to five days, depending on the course you are interested in. For more information on the Precept Ministries Institute of Training, call Precept Ministries.